Skiing

BY LAURA HAMILTON WAXMAN

AMICUS HIGH INTEREST • AMICUS INK

Amicus High Interest and Amicus Ink are imprints of Amicus
P.O. Box 1329, Mankato, MN 56002
www.amicuspublishing.us

Library of Congress Cataloging-in-Publication Data
Names: Waxman, Laura Hamilton, author.
Title: Skiing / by Laura Hamilton Waxman.
Description: Mankato, Minnesota : Amicus High Interest/
 Amicus Ink, [2018] | Series: Winter Olympic Sports |
 Includes index. | Audience: Grades: K to Grade 3.
Identifiers: LCCN 2016041970 (print) | LCCN 2017006957
 (ebook) | ISBN 9781681511511 (library binding) | ISBN
 9781681521824 (paperback) | ISBN 9781681512419
 (eBook)
Subjects: LCSH: Skis and skiing–Juvenile literature. | Winter
 Olympics–Juvenile literature.
Classification: LCC GV854.315 .W39 2018 (print) | LCC
 GV854.315 (ebook) | DDC 796.93–dc23
LC record available at https://lccn.loc.gov/2016041970

Editor: Wendy Dieker
Series Designer: Kathleen Petelinsek
Book Designer: Aubrey Harper
Photo Researcher: Holly Young

Photo Credits: Oliver Morin/AFP/Getty Images cover; PCN
Photography/Alamy Stock Photo 4; Yusuke Nakanishi/
Aflo Co. Ltd./Alamy Stock Photo 7, 11; Yohei Osada/Aflo
Co. Ltd./Alamy Stock Photo 8, 20; Kirsty Wigglesworth/AP
Photo 12; Mark Reis/Colorado Springs Gazette/MCT/Alamy
Live News/Tribune Content Agency LLC 15; Charles Krupa/
AP Photo 16-17; Clive Rose/Getty Images 19; Nick Atkins/
Actionplus/Newscom 22-23; Troy Wayrynen/ZUMA Press,
Inc./Alamy Stock Photo 24; Koji Aoki/Aflo Co. Ltd./Alamy
Stock Photo 27; Serfei Chirikov/epa european pressphoto
agency b.v./Alamy Stock Photo 28

Printed in the United States of America

HC 10 9 8 7 6 5 4 3 2 1
PB 10 9 8 7 6 5 4 3 2 1

Table of Contents

US skier Lindsey Vonn sprays snow as she skis down the mountain in the 2010 Olympics.

Going for Gold

The world's best skiers are here. They are ready to go head to head and wow the crowds. They cruise over the snow. They fly down the slopes. They soar off jumps. They twist and flip through the air. Ever since the first Winter Olympics in 1924, athletes have been skiing their hearts out for a chance at winning a gold medal.

Ski Jumping

A skier shoots down a ramp. She leaps off the edge. Then she sails through the air. Ski jumpers are scored on the length of their jumps. Their **form** in the air is judged, too. So is their landing. A smooth run wins more points.

Ski jumpers have thrilled crowds since the first Winter Olympic Games. But only men were allowed to jump. Finally in 2014, a women's event was added.

Women like Sara Takanashi
of Japan have proved their ski
jumping skills in the Olympics.

Skiers will sit on the colored bar as they get ready to slide down the normal hill.

 How far do jumpers soar?

There are three ski jump events. One event is on the normal hill, the smaller hill. Men and women compete on the normal hill. The other event is on the large hill. The top of that hill is higher. This means jumpers soar farther. There's a men's event and a team event on the large hill. Each team has four men. The team with the farthest jumps wins gold.

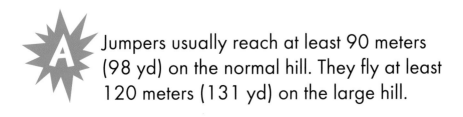

Jumpers usually reach at least 90 meters (98 yd) on the normal hill. They fly at least 120 meters (131 yd) on the large hill.

Cross-Country Skiing

Cross-country skiers face off in six different events. Two races are **sprints**. One sprint is for single skiers. The other is for teams of two. The teammates take turns skiing around a track several times. The **relay** is another team event. Four teammates take turns racing the course. The fastest team wins.

Men race in the cross-country
relay in the 2014 Olympics.

Gold medalist Marit Bjoergen of Norway is in the lead during the 2014 women's skiathlon.

 Are men's and women's cross-country events the same?

The two long-distance races take pacing. Skiers going too fast get tired quickly. But skiers going too slow get left behind.

The skiathlon is another long-distance event. Skiers race on **classical skis** for half the race. Then they switch to **skate skis**. These skis are shorter. This race tests skiers on two different ways to ski.

The rules of the events are the same. But most of the women's races are shorter distances than the men's.

Alpine Skiing

Whoosh! A skier flies down a steep, snowy **course**. Alpine skiing takes place on tall mountains. It takes balance, strength, and speed. The speediest alpine event is downhill skiing. It happens on the longest course. Skiers go into the **tuck position**. They pick up speed as they go. They must take wide turns without losing balance. The fastest time wins gold.

The downhill course has jumps that skiers must handle with control in order to win.

Slalom is another alpine event. The course is shorter and less steep than the downhill course. But the turns are much tighter. They are marked by dozens of **gates**. The skier must pass between the gates while keeping up speed.

The giant slalom is skied on a longer course. The gates are farther apart. This means the skiers can go a little faster.

US gold medalist Ted Ligety zooms down the giant slalom in 2014.

A fourth alpine event is the super giant slalom. It's often called super-g. This is the longest, steepest, and fastest slalom.

A fifth alpine event is the super combined. Skiers compete in a downhill run and a slalom run. Then their times are added together. The fastest skier wins the gold medal.

 Are there any other skiing events that combine two kinds of skiing?

Maria Höfl-Riesch of Germany takes a tight turn on the super combined slalom run.

 Yes! The Nordic combined is a ski jump and a cross-country race.

Freestyle skiing includes slopestyle.
Skiers twist and flip off of jumps
along the course.

Freestyle Skiing

Excitement rules in the freestyle events. In these events, skiers push the limit. They go over bumps and jumps. They do tricks high in the air. They race neck-and-neck.

In the aerial event, skiers glide down a long hill and sail off a jump. In the air, they do tricks. Judges score each skier's form. They give points for hard tricks and smooth landings.

Slopestyle and halfpipe began as snowboarding events. In 2014, Olympic skiers got in on the action. In slopestyle, skiers do tricks over jumps and obstacles down a slope. In the halfpipe event, skiers criss-cross down a pipe-shaped slope. They pop out of the pipe and do twists and flips. In both events, judges give high scores to the best style and most difficult tricks.

French skier Marie Martinod competes in the halfpipe.

Ski cross racers battle to win a high-speed race down the mountain.

The ski cross is another event that grew out of snowboarding. A ski cross course is a lot like a snowboard cross course. It's steep and curvy. It has turns, ridges, and jumps. Skiers race in groups of four. The two winners go on to the next round. In the last round, the fastest four skiers compete for the gold medal.

The moguls is the oldest freestyle event. It mixes skill and speed. A skier races down a steep, bumpy course. There are also two jumps. Skiers are judged on how well they handle the course. Do they have good form? How well do they handle the jumps and bumps? Speed is also part of their score.

 How old is freestyle Olympic skiing?

Japanese skier Aiko Uemara handles the bumps down the moguls course.

It started in 1992 with the moguls event. The other events were added in later years.

Catch the Excitement

Olympic skiing is a changing sport. A new team parallel slalom event is coming in 2018. Skiers from two teams race down the course at the same time. The team that wins the most of four runs moves to the next round. Keep your eyes on the slopes at the next Olympics!

The parallel slalom event has been part of the World Cup for years. Soon it will be an Olympic event.

Glossary

classical skis Long, cross-country skis that are parallel to each other.

course The slope or track a skier skies on in a skiing event.

form In skiing, the position of the body during a jump or trick.

gate In alpine skiing, a set of poles that a skier must ski between or around.

relay A team race in which each racer takes a turn doing one part of the course.

skate skis Shorter cross-country skis that are used more like skates.

sprint A fast, short race that requires a burst of speed.

tuck position A crouching position with bent knees and arms tucked close to the body.

Read More

Hunter, Nick. *The Winter Olympics*. Chicago: Heinemann Library, 2014.

Hunter, Nick. *The World of Olympics*. Chicago: Heinemann Library, 2012.

Trusdell, Brian. *Great Moments in Olympic Skiing*. Minneapolis, Minn.: Abdo Publishing, 2015.

Websites

Alpine Skiing: Winter Olympic Sports
www.olympic.org/alpine-skiing

TIME for Kids: Freestyle Skiing
www.timeforkids.com/news/freestyle-skiing/137701

US Ski Team
http://usskiteam.com/

Index

About the Author

Laura Hamilton Waxman has written and edited many nonfiction books for children. She loves learning about new things—like skiing—and sharing what she's learned with her readers. She lives in St. Paul, Minnesota.